AFFIRMATION

AFFIRMATION

POETRY FOR THE MIND & SOUL

VICTORY F. SHEPARD

authorHOUSE®

AuthorHouse™
1663 Liberty Drive
Bloomington, IN 47403
www.authorhouse.com
Phone: 1-800-839-8640

First published by AuthorHouse   07/25/2011

ISBN: 978-1-4634-2424-4 (sc)
ISBN: 978-1-4634-2423-7 (ebk)

Library of Congress Control Number: 2011909909

Printed in the United States of America

Any people depicted in stock imagery provided by Thinkstock are models, and such images are being used for illustrative purposes only.
Certain stock imagery © Thinkstock.

This book is printed on acid-free paper.

I would like to dedicate this book to the one who put this into my heart and soul and that is God Himself. I would not be able to do this without Him.

There are a few people who need to be thanked for their support.

My grandpa who always believed in me, I miss you.
My grandma who encourages me to follow my dreams,
I love you.
To my mom thanks for everything, and giving me courage,
I love you.
To my family, and friends who listened to me or cried with me or gave me words of comfort.
To Billy just remember your in my heart and prayers.
Val thanks for everything. Lets make the make the next twenty years or our friendship even more full of laughter.

Psalm 20: 4-5

Family Eph 1:5

Our Friendship

I remember the day we met,

way long ago in fourth grade.

You were this shy-little Michigan girl,

and I was this blonde-giggly desert rat.

The times we spent playing video games,

orlegos and barbie's at my house, a total blast.

I remember when you step-dad played the ken to our barbies

or when we watched Aerosmith's music video, 'Living on the Edge'.

The Beatles you first introduced me too,

while in return you put up with playing ponies with me.

I was inches shorter then you, even though I was older,

but when you wanted, you packed quite the spunk.

Laughter and tears life brought us both

and here we are twenty years later and still close.

You listen to my worries, dreams, and drama,

so in return I will help you beat Sonic the HedgeHog.

Let's continue our friendship long into the future,

and when that time comes I'll be the one pushing you will be pushing me
in my wheelchair

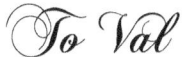

To Val

Friendship is

Friendship is a special bond
A bond often between many people
Whether newly aquired
Or one continued from childhood
A friend must be loyal
Someone to count on when needed
Friends listen to your worries and woes
They comfort each other in time of need
Friendship is also based on trust
Being there for each other when it counts
Dreams built off each other
From words of encouragement and that of critaism
Spilling each other secrets in total confidance
Bringing in a sense of calmness when life is rushed
Tears joys and so much more
Shared in the comfort of each others company
Friendship helps build us up or bring us down
Friends are family and sent to us from GOD.

Do you Know

Do you see what I see?
Do you know what I know?
Do you feel what I feel?
How can you say you know me,
when I am not you and you are not me.

Do you know what I am thinking?
Do you know my dreams?
Do you feels my pain?
How can you say that you know me,
when I am not you and you are not me.

Do you see through my eyes the world in view?
Do you even try to understand me at all?
Do you know my goals for my life?
How can you say that you know me,
when I am not you and you are not me.

Do you know why I do the things I do?
Do you even know what makes me tick?
Do you know what makes me weak or strong?
How can you say that you know me,
when I am not you and you are not me.

Do you know what goes through my head?
Do you know what makes my happy or laugh?
Do you know the simpleness that I love so dear?
How can you say that you know me,
when I am not you and you are not me.

Do you know my desire to worship the Lord?
Do you even understand what it is that I see?
Do you realize that I am a person too?
How can you say that you know me,
when I am not you and you are not me.

Did you know that my friends are people who love me for me?
And the ones you love except you for you?
Do you know why it is that I make the choices that I do?
How can you say that you know me
when I am not you and you are not me.

You say

So many people who say they are my friends

Say that they know me and it just never ends

And I am so tired of hearing what I need to do

When I am the one who knows and only God see me, not you

I should tell you that I am putting my foot down

And I will control my own choices and put on a grin instead of wearing this frown

I know you say that you want what is best for me

Well I will ask you one last time

Let me be who it is that God wants me to be

Can you please understand why I need my space

I am suffocating in this room and soon I will disappear without a trace

Just let me know that you are just there

And listen to what I need to say and let me know you care

So many times I have tried to be nice

Well I will only say it once and never again twice

I just want to live my life and not feel so drowned

I want to be feel happy like a queen when she is crowned

Thief in the Night

Constantly as the room turns
You wonder what future is to be
It is hard to loose someone you come to know
For anyone for you and even for me
I truly miss the one who was close to me
He died at such a young age
Leaving us with a question as to why
Feeling empty at a loss wanting to turn the next page
He was such a kind hearted soul
He always helped others, speaking the word of God
Trying as he may, we all knew he was ill
He never lied or portrayed that he was a fraud
Taken like a thief in the night
He is now happy and safe at his Maker's side
He left us with wisdom and a sense of place
So do not cover your eyes and try to run and hide
He reminded us of what we can really be like
That no matter what follow God, not you own will of heart
Live like you mean it and don't be left behind
For a new world awaits for you to start

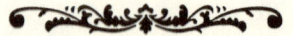

Mother your love

My mother that is who you are
only you and no other
Your smile brightens others around
no one else like you can be found
Your love and wisdom is unmatched
our bond forever secured and latched
Tears of laughter you bring to us all
you are always there to pick us up after we fall
You bring us faith in the darkest of times
and you have always put up with my poetic rhymes
Your family is the most important to you and you
are our families strong hold in all that we go through
You encourage myself and your son to follow our dreams
we know you are proud when your beautiful smile beams
Mother we love you more then we can express
more and more we wish to show and never any less

To my mom

Grandma you're the best

Grandma your awesome, you're the best
Great God did, when it was you He did invest
The stories and wisdom I will cherish, you see
I will remember all that you passed down to me
Beauty and strength I see in your eyes
Even with you worries, mistakes, fears and cries
Love and grace you have given to us all
The desire to dream and the courage to stand tall
Your family is all that it is, because of you
Because of your sacrifices and all that you went through
You're the start of it all, the Big Kahuna, the leader of the pack
Your love is never ending, never does is it lack
Your laughter I will hear always in my heart
No tears please grandma, now don't you start
You are a wonderful person both inside and out
You taught me what life means and what it's really about
Your faith in God is such an inspiration to me
And I hope and pray, like your faith, my faith will someday be
I know one day you'll be gone, on a date with grandpa I guess
Leaving behind memories and your sense of finness
I love you grandma I really do
You listen to me, in all that I go through
Thank you thank you for that you are
Jimminey Cricket is a saying I hear from you, so go ahead wish on a star

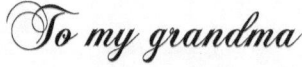

To my grandma

Never Alone

Even though you wait for your time to be free
I want you to know that you can lean on me
The bars of your cell I will bend to my will
I will listen to all that you say, taking in my fill
A friend I am and ever more through out our life time
Together we will overcome obstacles as we prepare for the final climb
No one can tell you that you are no good or that they don't care
I will always here to help, to listen, to share
Grab my hand as we escape life's prison of woes
Together we will journey unfolding the world's many hidden shows
Close the cell door to the past leaving it all behind
Lift your heart, your eyes open wide to every new find
Realize my dear you will be getting a second chance
Do not stay in one place long, do not be weary in your stance
Restless as you are strum the right key to get the right tone
And always remember dear one, you're never alone

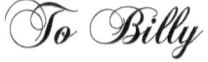

To Billy

The Family I have

Oh family, that is what we are
But to ever tell the stories behind our huge web of chaos you ask
I would need a whole slew of shrinks to listen to what we have been through
And that would be a very long running task

Every family has their up's and down's and in's and out's
But our faith is what brings us out and starting anew
We strive to better ourselves, despite what other's may think
We are a family, a unit, a sarcastic bunch, a full ships crew

No matter how crazy we may seem to everyone else
We are here for each other through hell and high water's
Easy going, still stubborn, sarcastic and so how still mellow
We help each other whenever in need we are not beggers, we are not flaunters

Take a look around I say
Thankful I am for the blessed family I have
They are who they are just as I am who I am
And I am thankful for who we are and what we have

Treasured Pearl

When is see you smile so sweet
You have the most adorable feet
Watching you grow is so hard to do
Yet I wouldn't be who I am with out you
Truly I was blessed to be your mother
I try not to spoil I really try not to smother
The first time I held you I felt such joy
And everytime I turn around I am buying you a new toy
To hear your laughter brings me a smile
For you I would walk more then a mile
My little girl I love you so much
When I first help you my heart you did touch
God has truly blessed me with such a beautiful baby girl
I wish to hold you close like a treasured pearl
And the day will come when you venture out on your own
I hope I taught you well, the whole world to be shown
I know one day you will grow and leave
The past we had is what I will want to retrieve
Tears I will cry when I give you away
Deep down inside though begging you to stay

To my daughter

13

Perfect Fit

To my dearest little girl
Having you as my daughter is beyond words
You are the light of my life in every way
I used to laugh histarically when you to catch the birds

The way you scrunch up your nose when you laugh
To the twinkle in your eye when you run to hug me
You run around so free and full of life
And you exactly the way God meant for you to be

Even when you are frustrated with your homework
To they way you throw a tantrum when you don't get your way
You have such a silly imagination deep down
You make me laugh at the you frolic and play

I like when you ask to tuck you into to bed
Or cuddle with me when either of us are feeling blue
I love when you tell how much you love me every day
Right down to the pictures you give me that you drew

You are my baby still no matter what you do
I couldn't see my life with out you in it
God really blessed me with you as my very own
Combined with our love, you and I are a perfect fit

To my daughter

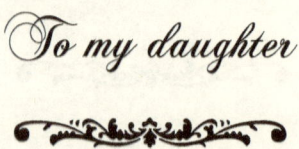

You Held Me

The first time I met you,
I knew you were meant to take my role
You were so kind to me, patient, understanding,
a woman with a lovely soul
Anticipated as you were to become a mother,
you still comforted me in my time of pain
The emotions that overtook me,
feeling as if I were hit twice by a train
Trusting you to be the mother,
that I knew I was not meant for them, to be
Even though I gave them life,
God always said you were their mother, not me
All the pieces of our meetings,
just seemed to fall into place
And my once tears of anger and jealousy,
God sought to replace
The bits and pieces of your personality,
reminded me a bit of my own
I remember the nervousness in your voice,
the first time we ever talked on the phone
You're their mother through all the good and bad,
the love that you hold for them with just one simple look
I hope one day you can sit down,
and read them the poems from me out of this book

I remember in the department store,

when I had to get away, and you knew why

You never seemed angry, nervous perhaps,

but you told me you could never replace me, then held me and let me
cry

Our tears both out of pain, joy, and mercy,

we connected that day, we connected as one

God brought us both together twice, in fact,

and mothers together, we love all three, our love shining as bright as
the sun

The Letters

I look over the letters
that you wrote so detailed and sweet
I close my eyes taking in a slow breath
trying not to tear up when I think of the day when we will once again
meet

It was destined by God's natural design
for our paths to cross even though we do not see each other
I reach for the photos of their darling faces
and smile because we are still so much apart of each other

The choices I had to make were so very hard
but I then remember no matter what I am their birth mother
A giggle I hear as I catch my little girl laughing
comparing herself to her baby sister and brother.

Preordained as the Lord saw fit
And no longer do I cry, questioning him as to why
You two were always there in my dreams long before we met
and I realize I am lucky to have you both, I softly sigh

Tears of happiness streak my face
as I think of how they are and the future to come
Such wonderful parents you both are, raising them as your own
even happy and nervous too, I bet, when finally explain where they come
from

And yes, one day soon we will meet again, soon I pray
and I know I will see all you loving faces
And their big sister will be waiting hand in hand
but only in the right times and the right places

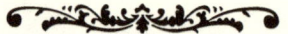

Precious Faces

I look over the pictures of your precious faces
And I ask my myself what you are like and what you will be
I love you both and miss you so much
And you both are still apart of my family tree

I wonder aloud what your favorite tv show is
Or what you like to play with or read
Your sister and her imagination I hope you both have
And just remember 'stick to your guns' that is our creed

I know that one day I will have a chance to see you both again
And I hope you understand that you will cry with me instead
I did not do this out of hate or greed
I wanted a better life for you both instead

Your eyes both so much like my own
Your curious and stubborn and both have a will of your own
Listen to me and listen with open ears
I did what I did out of love this is shown

Your parents love you and just as your sister and I do
And no matter what I am still here for the two of you when you need
So much I wonder what you both will think as you grow up
I did the best I could, I pray I did a good deed

Who you will become

The precious moments tick by
as i think of the day when i must say goodbye
Your eyes holding still holding so many so many questions for me
i know one day you will be a force for all the world to see
Good hearted and loving you always try to be
your future not yet founded still so young and carefree
Worries overwelm me as i think of who you will become
hoping that you remember where you come from
Joys and laughter you bring into my world each day
your dreams coming true i hope and pray
God made you who you are HIS own individual design
your character and personality others do not decline
You are who you are sarcasm and all
you will continue to make mistakes but you will learn from each fall
Creative you are a kind hearted soul
the future awaits for you to one day take on your own role

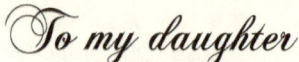

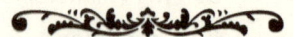

Nature Mt 8:25

Together we stand

Together we should stand
in or order to protect this wonderful land
We cut and unearth every tree root
Money in the pockets of some rich man's suit
We must endure the damage we cause
Most of us don't blink let alone a moment to pause
There are always ways to preserve this planet for our future
A way to fix the damage, a way for us to suture
Recycle and focus on what must be done
Don't sit back, letting the suit make money thinking they've won
Fight for the right of the planet you see
Lets teach, help, and learn for the planet for you and for me
Taken for granted, torn peace by peace, at such a cost
Gather together, before all is lost
We only get this planet for as long as we are here
But the future is dim, for the next generations i fear
Behold nature in all its wonder and majestic glory
Give this planet a chance, a place for the next generations to tell their story
I have to cry at all we have done, so unjust
Although the Bible says we will once again return to the earth as dust
Be prepared for what nature throws back at us
One day, you'll see, all will be as it one was

Welcoming in the Night

The sun is setting
And I sit wondering
What the next day brings
Hope and wonders
Brilliant in the creator's image
The bringing of such transitional peace
The cool wind blows
Crickets sounding with such a chorus
Welcoming in the night
I scrunch my toes
Into the soft sand beneath
The power and peace as nature was meant to behold
Soft sounds in the distance
Saying that the night will soon be here
Bringing with it, the curiosity to explore
Stars begin to appear in the night sky
As the sun begins to fade
Painting an array of colors across the setting sky
The chaotic hum in the hustle and bustle
Of our daily routine lives
Echoing somewhere in the distance
As the last bit of sun sets in the sky
I rise to my feet glancing back once
Goodbye to the peaceful day and hello to the whispering night

Earth's unleashed furry

I watch in tears as the earth unleashes its rousing furry
Everywhere all around people trying to get away in a hurry
There is no safe haven on this planet to hide
Nature is all we see, now open your eyes wide
Our technology can not really save us in the end
That is our mistake in which we all depend
Most of us ignore the panic, turning our heads the other way
Thinking of the future, what about tomorrow or next day
Volcano's erupt, that experts say laid dormit
You were not around during creation and you did not form it
Yet here we are as the earth rumbles and shakes
The earth will do as it always has done, despite the high stakes
Animals have the internal instinct to hide or flee
And still all around, nature will unleash all we continue to see
Storms will pour down rain drowning us in water, no more dry land
People uprooted like a snap of a band
We can help recover what has been lost
Pouring over rubble, rummaging through what a tornado tossed
Human, animals and nature must learn to live together
Despite the risks, even when earth unleashes its powerful wheather

Flash for Flash

Lightning is beautiful
As it flashes across the night sky
Dangerous it may also be
Still entrancing me with its magnetic shows
Thunder soon follows after the strike
Leaving me shaking down to my boots
Storms are such a wonder to me
As rain pours down, pouring down on all I see
The brilliant flash of light
Nearly close enough to strike down my tree
Follow I must, I must see
To capture the power current of pure electricity
A picture I claim is all I want
Still the storm moves on ahead, not waiting for me
The smell of rain fills the air
Calm and peaceful as I feel the first drops
Wind carrying the world in every whisper
As it gains speed, nearly knocking me down
Lightening once again strikes
And this time much closer, do I even dare try
One shot that all I need
Flash for flash, captured, for all to see

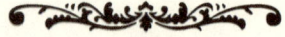

A rare find

Iused to have this very cool cat

She was a pretty kitty and oh yeah she was really fat

She was the only cat i knew that liked to take bath you see

Once she even jumped into the bath with me

Most cats look like a drown rat, not her, a solid mass of fur

She was different how she would play attack the feet to her really loud purr

Once when we were all eating and watching tv

Her way of thinking was 'i am hiding in plain sight but you can't see me'

Out came her one claw as she slowly snatched the chicken off my brother's plate

Him watching her as she thought he took her 'you can't see me' bait

And she had a sense to not like tuna but she sure liked to eat human food

And forget about me doing homework shed plop down and i would say excuse me how rude

She even had this show she had to watch at the same time everyday

Bear in the big blue house and she would lay on the remote to make sure the channel did stay

She was stubborn as she was really fat

Oh how i miss that silly cat

She did not like the sound that the crickets made

So she would tear off their back legs and for annoying her, this was the price they paid

It sounded like thunder when she came down the stairs

And if she knew you were sad she snuggle to show she cares

Then was this fact that she opened any door if she wanted

Or play tag with my baby girl whenever she wanted

Her personality was one of a kind

My cat she really was a rare find

She really went with up where ever we went

Whether or not we lived in a house motel car or tent

Once my mom was making dinner and our she climbed into the fridge to find something to eat i guess

An hour later my mom found her there, cold, but full leaving behind no mess

Loosing a pet can leave you empty and filled with sorrow

But my cat would want me to look for a better tomorrow

I miss her i will admit that

I really do miss that sarcastic and stubborn cat.

Loving as dolphins

When you see a dolphin
what is it you see
I see a calmness deep within
bringing out an inner peace and serenity

To see them up close
to be able to swim with them as they frolic and play
To hear their mysterious songs
no matter what time of day

They have a sense of humor and a constant playfulness
as you study them from a distance
Happy you feel as you begin to laugh
and calm and at peace to say for instance

The soothing ocean is their home
for they are in the open and totally free
To see their world through their echo location
to be apart of them and apart of the sea

So many dangers threaten them in this world
trying to bring about this enchanting creatures end
As playful and loving as dolphins may be
they need our help they need up to help defend

Victory F. Shepard

There mystical creatures
are apart of who we are and earths future
help bring an end to their butchered end
instead help to mend heal and sutture

Ultimate Race Track

A horse noble in his stance
Heart pounding as i catch a second glance
Beautiful red mane my fingers must touch
A glory to heaven i wish to ride so much
Sacred i feel at the power of the huge beast
A coward will i never try once to say the least
Hooves pounding the dirt with such power wanting to race
Intelligant and beauty in his magnificant face
Eyes that hold wisdom looking around i begin to wonder
To hear him run is like hearing the roaring of thunder
I step back to take in all that i see
Such strength no weakness with such natural grace to me
Tame is not a word meant for him that i stand before
Give him wings for freedom and he will soar
Carefully i run my hands softly over his muscled back
Speed agility stamina for the ultimate race track
Freedom and space i wish to grant him and more
instead in comes the keeper behind him closing the door
My heart aches as this captive creature watches me with pleading eyes
Let him go i must to run through heavens natural green skies
I look over my shoulder then quickly and carefully climb on his back
Together we shall head to the ultimate race track
He moves so in step and one with the earth
Steady and paced just as this fine horses birth

He signals to me in his patient but weary stance that he is ready
open the door now holding together a beat strong and steady
Hearts racing as one as he stop without any slack
Freedom he cries as we at last head for the ultimate race track

Huntress of the night

Her silky black fur glistening under the moonlight
Her eyes watchm her prey ever so close
She readies herself preparing to pounce
Fur as black as midnight CAMAFLAUGING her with the dark
Claws contracting for the final attack
Her quiet stalking closing in for the kill
Eyes targeting as she tears into the night.
Her prey sensing danger a little to late
Her powerful act reflexes quick and precise as she gracefully runs
Her prey one step to slow as she swipes him with her claws
The strength of her jaws as she strangles him of his last breath
The bloody capture awaits now silent in front of her
Her content purr loud as she dines under the glowing light of the moon
She has brought herself satisfaction skillfully at the end
She is the black panther the invisible and dark hunttress of the night

Curious Universe

The universe
is curious as we are
In all its beauty
and continued vastness
So many wonders
are out there to find
Its many hidden secrets
we strive to unlock
The galaxies creating
new chamber to explore
Making up question whether
there is life some where out there elsewhere
Our planet in its orbiting place
in this wast universe
Is among a rare
and purpose made design
We stare at the stars above
so far away
Letting us know that we are
our individual lives are unique
Calm the universe seems
from our own home planet

Cosmic and powerful
in all its vast wonder
Dreams of exploring space
creating new ideas in a childs mind
And still we know and sense
that we are all here for only a short time

Nature in all its magic and glory

Nature in its magic and glory
Is beautiful to gaze upon
The soothing sound of the sea
As its waves crash into the shore
The beautiful display and wonder
as the lava washes down the side of a volcano
The wind how it blows and never seen
Making music for us or bringing silence to our ears
A waterfall as majestic as it flows
Creating a beautiful decor with its color of rainbows
The trees around standing tall and firm
Reminding us remember of this peaceful place
The tornado even though leaving havoc in its wake
From a distance mesmerizing us with its hypnotic dance
The clouds swirling above to soft and serene
Create a vision of heaven if that is what you believe
A hurricane strong and forceful in its constructive ploy.
The shore and sea meeting crash for crash creating their own symbolic
ritual
So many words can be said for what is seen
Only few people give it a chance and only few make a sound

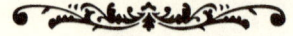

Still Heated Desert Place

The heat is intense
in this desert place.
Water evaporates
under the got suns rays.
Creatures hide from this place
seeking shade until the night
Scarce is life in the daylight
of this baron and vast desert land
The sun bears down heating up
this landscapes surface
Sweet tasting water
no where in sight to be found
Dizziness swept up
under exhausting heat of the sun
No sound to be heard
not even a slither of a rattlesnake
Shade a rare find searching
on a neverending journey
Scarce is the food
aware of lifes many hungers
Rather to be drowned
than teased under this desert heat
More and more of the suns rays charge over
bringing the temperature hotter

Victory F. Shepard

Prayer for the night to come
to cover this baron land in darkness
To them cast shadows forbidden
in the rays of the light of the sun
Coming is the sunset finally
bringing out the creatures of the night
The quiet is no more
in this still heated desert place

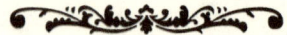

Bringing change anew

I listened in tears as i heard of the passing tornado
leaving behind havoc a town ripped in half by its wake
though the town is still apart of the historic route of the past
nothing left to recognize leaving those who pass by in shock
people wonderin how they move on from this disaster
so much lost debree covering the now nameless streets
confusion and panic questioning what is next
many now dead and still searching for store missing
in so little time nature caused such a travesty
still time passes on bringing a lingering hope
yesterday forever gone tomorrow ready to begin
the newness can bring a secret inner peace
there is many still picking up the shattered pieces
faith is stirring just around the next bend
be tearful for those we now mourn
pray for those who still wait to be found
do not let this happening bring about the end of this town
GOD is helping to rebuild all lost for those who believe
and trying to bring comfort for those who are lost and in need

To the city of Joplin

His world in need

look around at what i see
a much bigger picture of the whole world around me
So much i wish to travel and to search
to spread HIS word a missionary for GODS earthly church
You see not only was HIS word meant for us
dont you see HIS world in need we need to focus
He put up on this planet to grow and to learn
HE made this planet for us to harvest the soil for food in turn
This planet is in need of help for our own survival
we must all come together to help in earths revival
See the work of GOD in the beauty HE created in nature
instead of putting this earth through our consistant torture
Spread HIS word for the whole earth as well
this planet was created for us not for up to debate over and sell

Patriotic suit

Somedays I wonder if dedication is what we lack

The fighting and pettiness, after our country was under attack

Open your eyes, to full view you don't have to search hard for the clue

We have our problems, as everyone in the world does, is this not true?

We have a great nation that is worth fighting for

But it must be honest and loyal, but instead we treat it as a chore

First we must fix ourselves and our drastic way of thinking

For the captain nor the crew are aboard, they left us all sinking

Our whole world is chaotic in one way or another

One day I pray peace will prevail, instead of constantly fighting each other

Please now, get up, use your mind, how do we make it better?

Sing a song, promote positive attention, in any case you can always write a letter

We complain and wine about all these rules and our unfair laws

It's the blind leading the blind into the strength of the dragon's claws

We need a mighty herd of knights to be brave and stand firm

Slay the dragon of injustice, leaving little to squirm

Let's take a quick peek into the future, at what we may be able to do

We are all apart of this country and its making, so come to

Forgive those around, get over our pity, move forward from the past

A bright new future for the sake of our land, we must help to make it last

Show your red white and blue colors, put on your patriotic suit

Be brave, as said 'all men are created equal', lets strengthen this root

Our next generation

My heart is crying
when I see the constant fighting
we must open our eyes
despite the ever pour lighting
our next generation looks to us
to show them the next step
courage and faith
into their future we must prep
to teach them and guide them
prepare them to continue the fight for peace
we lead them they look to us
so no more fighting let is all cease

Love Gn 19:24

Lucky Mother

Such a wonder to me
is a mother to be
life growing with in
a new hope about to begin
wonder and beauty all rolled in
one joy as bright as the sun
two hearts beating together
every storm they will whether
every new step a new and different wonder
your loving heart beating like thunder
as the time slowly passes
ready the bottles and wine glasses
here soon comes your darling infant
you are so calm in an instant
a mothers love soon spilling over
lucky she feels like a four leaf clover.

Presious new life

so precious this new life she holds
tiny little hands and such tiny little toes
tears flow over, joy warming her heart
today she undstands the meaning of love
the word mother move then just just a word on a page
the meaning of life now asleep in her arms
bringing a new hope for tomorrow and into the future
the precious baby wakes letting out a newborn cry
tears well up in the mothers eyes once again
this precious newborns life is now dependant on her
a smile glows upon her face as she kisses her babys soft face
a mystery the bond between mother and child
her babys footsteps she will follow closely behind
a journey until then as they travel down their path in life

Dreamless Sleep

The midnight hour slowly ticks by
Finally launching me into a restless slumber
As I enter the world of the empty dreamland
Often my dreams chaotic and twisting with the beat of a circus tumbler

I see myself in there in strange and far off places
And I wonder if it is real or pretend
These sleepless dreams are filled with sorrow
And I wonder will this dream never end

In these strange dreams they are often filled with silence
And I worry that the echo of the silence will drive me crazy
To many times I have tried to run and hide in the mist
But all around me is blurred visions and memories are hazy

Why is it when I try to remember its out of my grasp
And the sorrow of the lost dream brings me sudden empty pain
The moon still shines and my dreams still chaotic
All I wish is to remember this dreamless sleep to remain sane

Forget the days events as I recall the visions of silent sleep
Filled with no real dreams, no waking sorrow to disturb my deep slumber
Nothing to wake me, nothing at all, no noise, not a peep
So I have to ask, why this dreamless sleep, I wonder?

The Charade

What i see when i look into your eyes
is your twisted distortion of truth into lies
I talk but you do not hear the words i say
and i walk to you as a servant my words left empty on the tray
Alone i feel day after day and still i wait
pondering a solution to help set us straight
Together is not a word i often hear anymore
no longer do i seek or even know what i an looking for
I do not know why i continue this charade
i see the vision of us begin to fade
Why is it you are so blind as to all you do
after all this time after all we have been through
No longer do i have a sense of reality with you
you took all i had and all i once knew
No longer do i even know what brought us together
and no more do i believe when you promise me forever
How did this happen to us how did we get here
bitterness and anger will follow us both i fear
Seperate paths soon we must both choose
or sadly my dear in the and we shall both loose

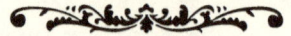

My Promised Forever

I dream of him night after night
I dream of my promised forever
I wait for my path to be set right
In reality he is not here, not ever
I cry and wake to the feeling of empty hopes
In my dreams he holds me close, my promised forever
I climb and climb trying to not fall from these ropes
Still man of my dreams, you're a dream, not really here, whatever
His eyes as dark as this hole inside of me
Oh where are you, where, my promised forever
You whisper dreams of how you will let me free
I call out to you, you don't hear, not ever
A joke I play, a fool's wish on my own heart
But still I want you near, my promised forever
Will this universe destine us forever apart
These dreams I have, I choose to not sever
A spark of hope still lingers, somewhere in me
And I begin to hope once more, of my promised forever
Though in my dreams you still remain, and you hear me cry for thee
I will not give up my dream love, I will never give up, never

My Apollo

You bring light into my life
Banishing the shadows back into the dark
As you smile down upon me, my Apollo

The joy I feel when your around
Fills my heart with music of love
Play you lyre and sing me your song, my Apollo

As I lie here with your strong arms around me
You whisper me promises and desires, and hopes
Continue, your voice as soft as the wind, my Apollo

I close my eyes trusting in our embrace
As the world around us is lost
Our love seems to fall into place, my Apollo

I dream of you late into the night
As you cherish our time and love, you write
Your poetry, dear love, could fly me to the moon, my Apollo

I smile to myself as our fingers interlace
I do not wish for our time to end
Tell me what does our future hold, my Apollo

I wish to only stay right here
In you embrace safe and unbroken
You kiss my cheek as my tears pour out, my Apollo

You tell me in words of courage and faith
That our love will not end and we shall see each other again
Your words will remain in my heart along with you, my Apollo

As the morning sun shine so bright
You speak only a word mending the pieces of my once broken heart
You are my sun rise, and my eternal dream, my Apollo

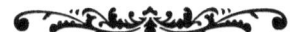

Alluring Brown Eyes

As i stare dreamily into your alluring brown eye
s feeling once again as a school girl full of anticipation and suprise.
Still your soft brown eyes stay focused straight ahead
music in the night as your voice lulls me soundly in my bed.
Trying as i might to not drift off into a lazy sleep
i hear the echo of your voice fade into slumber i fall and deep.
The visions in my dreams bring me sorrow and tears
and it is that i must soon wake that brings me fears.
I wish to only stay in your silent embrace forever
no longer wanting to return to the real world ever.
I know that dawn approaches as i slowly awaken
distant dreams a blur but still have left me quite shaken.
As the sun rises setting hope in for a new day
i close my eyes sighing maybe maybe someday.
The sound of your voice fills the morning air
to fall back to sleep to dream of you do i dare.
Your a dream a vision a costant hope
a dream i know time is slow in my own tv soap.
I know that this is not real and it hurts me so much.
To just once to see you in real life to feel our fingertips touch.

A Rockstar

How did this happen your a fantasy i soppose

so why is it i am not bringing this all too real dream to a close.

Why is it that a fall victom to some celebrity crush

my heart racing as my thoughts torturing me with this fiery rush.

Please take back these days of constant daydreams

your eyes setting fire straight to my heart burning me at the seams.

Soft and warm brown eyes always watching over me

please in leave me alone no more wanting dont you see.

I am not a foolish silly hearted girl as i once was

but you bring back this fluttery feeling that i cant ignore and this is because.

Please i beg show mercy on me i cry and i plead

why is it you way be my white knight riding up on your trusty steed.

I no longer wish to fancy over someone i will never see

no more of the butterflies in my stomach or my heart buzzing as a bee.

I fall to the floor emotions and confusion overwelming me.

I feel shaken and lost for all the world to see.

As i glace away from your face to outside and afar.

I ask myself how is it i fell in love with a rockstar.

Quickly i will refresh myself letting no one to see me in this state

and again i will dream only in the end to wait and wait.

That moment

Our eyes lock
as motions are set into place
Unsure of the next move
as i mentally etch every curve of your face
The steady beat of my heart setting pace
as you continue to gaze at me from across the room
A link i feel we momentarily share
or so i assume
Still i trace the movements of your lips
as you continue to have your ever set eyes on me
A sudden peace flows through me
as i continue to stare down my new inner chi
A sound from somewhere around
brings us both back into focus
I look down this moment in time
no longer trying to entrance us
I hear the laughter as i look up
just in time to see you leave
A moment i pause waiting
for a silent signal that i wish to receive
You do not look back
instead you walk casually out the door
A voice inside secretly wanting that moment
to rewind for just a second more

Reality sets its place as my friends
move to our new spot in line
For a second time shifted in that momen
as our fates did intertwine

Sing your Song

in all the universe
your love is absolutely cosmic
You look like a dream
your words singing of every scandelous topic
Stars collide so high above
as you enter or exit a room
All eyes follow you in everything you do
and you smile brings about a sudden bloom
The moon flashes brightly
in the night sky
reminding the flames
in your eyes to ignite
Words smoothly pour out as you sing your song
and attention is focused on you tonight
Galaxies silent in their existance
and the earth comes to a stop for i time
In slow motion i forget to take in i breath
as your solar flare voice brings my heart to a climb
As the earth spins so do I
as your voice brings star kissed tears to my eyes
The moon light once again ignites your already turbulant gaze
the song ends you bow retreating triumphant in your goodbyes

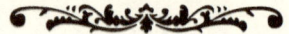

Treasoned Heart

I remember the first time
i ever laid eyes on you
I fell in that moment
forbidden this i always knew
The words you speak
when you speak of HIM above
Gives of the inspiration
the passion to seek out such love
A man yes you are
but a rare find for the moment
And it brings me to tears
this rage of forbidden torment
A glass shield i keep
to protect myself at an enclosed distance
But when i needed you there
you were for me in an instance
Why do these rules bind
to what is securely in place
I wish to have my heart run free
to finally reaching that home base
I know the reasons that will keep us
forever only inches apart
And do not want to admit
that i had fell from the start

Victory F. Shepard

I do no longer want to to see your blue eyes
or to hear your words voice reason
I will stay away
but to my own heart i must commit treason

Love is often

love for any of us
can be a hard find
but we must never give up
keep a postive frame of mind
love is a feeling acted out
for not just pleasure
it is an emotion an spoken
truly we must treasure
love is often overspoken overthought
not comprehending the meaning
it is a world that needs
to be taken out of text for a cleaning
love is not obsession
but is rhythmic with your heart
love is redeeming
letting each the freedom to be apart
love is not said for an object
but rather a person instead
love is whole hearted
a pause for the words that must be said

As my own daughter

I remember the moment I walked into your hospital room
this time joy thundered through me instead of lurking doom
I watched you hold him your first born son
motherhood maturing you despite all you have done
I watched you grow and learn lifes hard lessons
trying as I did with advice only for you in good intentions
but there I stood a daughter to me deep in my heart
knowing you would okay in your life from the very start
the love I saw pour from you as your held you son close
he looks so much like you even down to your nose
now here we are a year later down the road
a mother I feel towards you years of joy from my heart ready to explode
you both are perfect as mother and her son
life's journey for both of you has only just begun

To my adopted daughter and her son

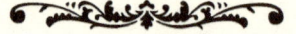

Unlimited Extensions

Affirmation is defined as a moment
thougt or a single frame of mind
with these affirmations can com and rare
moment learned in time or altering life long lessons
Whatever the reason for a new found inspiration
it can lead to on an adventure to our own inner find
with every affirmation there is something gained
without understanding its realised good intentions
one may come during a moment of trials
but can change our hearts for something we once pined
Many can be from God Himself
giving faith and His unlimited extentions

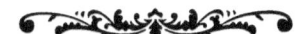

Filled with empty promises

All the time i feel i think of you both
day in and day out
You feel my dreams with empty promises
and angrily i want to shout
Although the sky is more blue
when we walk hand in hand
When i stumble or fall
you are right there to help me stand
But my dreams are empty and i know
they could never come to pass
Romantic you are always in these dreams
always as you sweetly hand me my wine glass
A soft hope and whispering chances
as i wish for this dream to became real
Alas it is only a empty dream
and tip is my eternal deal
Still i will hold onto you
the man of my forever dreams
One day i will have a love
so close to you or so it seems
He is out there somewhere
i hope to meet him someday soon.
And we shall walk along the shore
somewhere by the light of the moon

You may be only a dream
in the true sense but what i seek to find
Made up of what i want and alot of what i need
but for now a dream in my mind

Faith 2 Kings 6:16-17

True Holiday Cheer

Little ornaments hang from the tree.
Letting up know the holiday we see
Taking every little thing in our lives for granted.
These brilliant seeds were long ago planted.
Gifts stores always say bring holiday cheer.
Every morning when you wake take a glance in the mirror.
Forgotten the true reason we all celebrate.
When the end is near it will be to late
hold your family friends and neighbors close.
For hugs HE who died for up and three days later HE rose.
Snow falls on the streets with the bringing of new hope
HIM letting us know that we will not slip off this rope.
A hug or an honest act of charity we see.
As we all gather round the shimmering tree.
We seem to say that we want this or we want that.
And when HE knocks HE is left standing on the door mat.
Born to us from our loving father above.
He bled for our sins to show us HIS love.
Take your child by the hand.
Time is precious like a single grain of sand
Remember what the true holiday spirit means.
For our father is watching up closely from behind the scenes.
Focus on the true spirit of holiday cheer.
For it comes around once in a single year.

These Personal Crossroads

Many times in life we feel as if we stand alone

God gave us free will letting our choices be our own

Look in the mirror closely what do you see

God made you His personal creation and who you will be

So many times we all stand taking the easy the way out

Why choose easy be bold show some spunk don't moap and pout

We all stand eventually in from of a fork in the road

Choices where shall I go some choose to take it easy with their load

Worn is the path they walk greading behind others before

Those who choose and hard is this path where they become history's lore

Traveling is hard and is this path where footsteps are barely made out

More fulfilled happy living the dream making them who they are about

These many personal crossroads are always throughout our lifetime

Leading us towards courage untold or pretending all talk reall the mime

Take the chance God will be there for me and you

Strike out live really be happy with God be true

I am Yours

God you have blessed me with so much

me even with my flaws and mistakes

i cry every night pain etches the layers of my heart

Your love is unfathomable i could never know

all i know is You carry me through despite everything that has happened

i pray and praise all Your love and forgiveness

truly You are a wonderful GOD and You deserve all my love and prais

days are brighter with You in my heart

and nights are not lonely with You next to me

tears wash over my face at the blessing You do give

i still dont understand why You love me so

i am wicked by nature and stubborn by will

and yet You fill me with Your love and mercy

LORD You are great in all You do

Your creation is i sight to behold

You knew me still in my mothers womb

You know me both inside and out

i feel lighter when i give You all my worries

and lighter still with Your love flowing through me

praise i give You creator of heaven and earth

i am Yours all Yours oh LORD.

He Died

In the darkness You shine Your light.

Leading the way Your love so bright.

I drop to my knees to worship You.

You have up Your blood Your life too.

The wind blows calmly all around me.

I know that i am not even worthy for Thee.

Faithful as i really try to stay.

Temptation trys to lure me the other way.

Coldness brings my body to a chill.

I know it is Your word i should will.

Strength and compassion and mercy all come from You.

If only people weren so blind if only they knew.

Kindness is not a sign its an act.

He died for us that is our pact.

Child of darkness come around.

Come towards the light kneel to the ground.

All is well in the house of the LORD.

Yet people will still pick up their sword.

Run towards the swaying tree.

For HE is there waiting for you and for me.

Rain begins to fall from the sky.

Mud covers the land we must press on we must try.

I do fear what could happen to my soul.

I an also afraid to take on this new role.

Without Fear

Alone no longer i feel as i stand in this place of white sand

i am here awaiting the promised land

traveling i did such a long way

waiting watching wanting to stay

i sit and wait for HIM to once again show

suns heat casting down no cool wind to blow

i close my eyes to hear their song

admitting silently that all i knew was wrong

tears begin to shower down my face

HE wipes them away leaving no trace

tired my soul feels ready for flight

i stare deeply into the moonlit night

waiting for with HIS arms open wide

He shows me the people who truly lied

He stands and walks to cliffs edge

showing HIS scars and what HE did pledge

He does not have to speak a word to me

HE points to the heavens to make me see

i cry aloud but He pulls me near

the clouds begin to part and i will enter without fear

i look back to see HIM smile and nod a chance i see

i will follow HIM and i shall wait for the day when HE comes for me

Lifes Battles

I stare at my reflection in the mirror
still trying to brace myself for lifes battles.
I feel the loom of threat as it nears
as the earth itself shakes and rattles.
comfort at the end of the day is what i seek
Not wanting to open that door to face another day.
Still i pick up my sword and shield
and say a prayer to not be led astray.
Lost i already feel in a world of constant commotion
while technology DROWNS out the peace and calm of nature.
No more i scream as i yell into the mirror
no more chaos and suffering i must endure.
The protective hum of my armor is loud as i ready myself
i close my eyes as i pick up the sword of truth.
Each day passing by me in a blink of an eye
with my new found armor of faith i feel as powerful as i did in my youth.
Knowledge and wisdom have to very OPPISITE definitions
just as understanding and comprehending have two different meaning.
Still as i breath in slowly now ready to walk firmly for my battle
my mind is clear and alert after my spiritual cleanings.
I only know one fact deep down in my heart
LORD You are always standing right next to me.
You hold the enemy back as i begin to venture out
i trust in what You taught me LORD not in what i see.

The battle of my life will soon enough come to a halt
when the earth declares HIM as rightful LORD and king.
One day i will happily set down my battle gear
and we will gather to praise you as the angels chorus of you they will
sing.

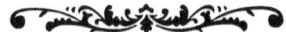

Why Not Believe

Do you believe a man can walk on the moon.

Then why not believe in the LORD of all creation.

Do you believe in love at first sight.

Then why not believe in the One who loves up all

. Do you believe that there can be peace throughout the whole world.

Then why not believe in the One named prince of peace.

Do you believe in giving your life for another.

Then why not believe in the One who gave us HIS life.

Do you believe you are one in a million.

Then why not believe in the One who knew you while still in your mothers womb.

Do you believe in the innocence of a young child.

Then why not believe in the One who calls us His children.

Do you believe that good will over throw all evil.

Then why not believe that HE will always prevail.

Do you believe in everlasting life.

Then why not believe in HIM who can give you everlasting life.

Comic Book Life

My stomach feels sucker punched my
head given a double WHAMMEY.
I feel unknowingly nervous
slightly feverish and definately clammy
i remember that saying
when push comes to shove
but i know i will make it trough this crowd
for i seek Your everlasting love.
I must stop feeling anxious
and turn to You now
before my life turns into a comic book
for all to read to late kerplow.
Most of the time i feel like inspector gadget
with a good intended mix up or goof
and when i am without You
LORD i am lost that is the proof.
Circle Your mercy and compassion
around me in Your light of eternal love
GOD i realize now You have been here from the start
i held my head down low instead of looking above.

Mirrored Image

Every day when I look in the mirror
I see a shadow of who I once was
My faith wavers in and out
And I feel as if I am in a disco
I step out into the sunlight
My spirit ready to really start anew
As I gaze around around at my desert homeland
I catch a glimpse of someone coming towards me
Who would this be walking in thisf intense heat
I move slowly forward to call out to them
In an instant they seem to copy my every move
Shock runs through as I realize the truth
It is nothing but a potrayed mirage
False int its image it mirror my moves
That is not me I am not here here, not now
My heart beat drums loudly in my ears
I am deaf as I scream for someone to help
Sitting quickly upright in the comfort of my bed
I wipe the seat off my brow, a dream
No not a dream a vision holding to much truth
I throw the covers back as I kneel to the floor
Clasping my hands and bowing my head in prayer
I ask myself why am I still lingering here
Lost in my own dester searching forever
I do not know what hold me back
Realization crosses over me as I begin to cry

To much of my past I hold onto too why

Hidden in the shadows behind humiliation and fear

Lord I beg pull me through

Forgeveme for not letting go I must must let go

The face of my fear comes into view

I wish only to quickly retreat, oh Lord, what do I do?

You must face this part of yours i know

how how can You ask me to forgive to forgive so easily

the pain and anguish i so solemly went through

bidding time but the while forever holding back words

the embarrassment and torment the anger and rage

balling my fists at my side i slowly stand to my feet

my heart beat thundering in my ears

no more i say through clenched teeth

Lord help me give me the words to say

taking in a breath i whisper into the quiet darkness

i will forgive you and i really mean i do

relief sweeps through me as the weight is lifted

i pour out my tears as i release my anger

thank You LORD where would i be without You

once forever lost in my own sorrow and pity

forgiveness its so very hard to do

but without it i could not live in your light Lord with You

i would be lost and empty

no light shining on me LORD You are here You are to pull me through

His Initial Plan

I try to walk with HIM
with a positive attitude
Instead of quickly trying
to retreat to my fortress of solitude
He is with me everyday
in all that i do
So easy could i well and curse
and blame HIM for all i have been through
But them i sit back thinking
a second to pause
This is what the devil wants
to capture me in the strength of his jaws
It almost tempts me to laugh
and watch the show unfold
But i have a chance a deal
that I must uphold
Keep focus in front of me
stay on track
I must pick up my cross
never falter never slack
He is here for us to be here
so that our future is not so dim
He is our Father in heaven we must believe in Him

New Day Dawns

When i lay awake at night

with destiny and self pity a constant fight

question lingers in the back of my head

fear and anguish sorrow anger and dread

this path that i so foolishly chose

is that i bring to a close

taken my spirit it has gone away

leaving me alone in the mist walking astray

i fall to my knees asking You Lord for forgiveness

lead me away from all this constant drearyness

as a friend did once say to me

i must help down the path of our destiny

the child i hold looks at me and cries for hope

i have let to loosely from this rope

i need help to answer my heart

Lord for You can read my mind

what is the answer

to thequestion of truth that i must find

along the way i saw HIM

as HE stood there

waiting to lead me but to where

HE is there always

watching over me

even when my faith lacks

why cant i just let things be

When i look in the mirror

i see only a shadow

and i feel that

Victory F. Shepard

somewhere i am above
and i am watching
myself below
the sins of my past
shall be no more
our new life ahead
that is what we hope for
she looks at me for just
comfort and love
i wish i could but i feel
no real peace comes with my dove
my happyness slowly melting
but a light still flickers
and no more taunt
s sneers or smickers
i clearly watch this woman
let the child leave with in
a new day dawns our lives
ready to finally begin
my little girl to not worry
do not sad
get up with me
let us be glad
for Your love LORD
casts all our shadows away
i smile with her standing next to me
the glimmer of hope dawns a new day

Your own true Worth

Everyone of us at a loss for hope drowning no words left to speak

While the enemy sits there quiet and patient to find what makes us weak

Broken and bound loosing all sense of peace and the sense of ones own reality

We must leave control to HIM Who is the Maker and the Bringer of peace and serenity

His words inscribed with all of our lifes questions and prayers

We should not get caught up in the evil being led along into the confines of evils layer

Light and love HE wishes to bring into our empty and forboding hearts

Forever HE is with us sing and shout as this new day starts

We shall drown in the mercy and blessings of HIS unfathomable love and grace

The plot against evil and his minions to be set their place

Together all we are is through HIM CHRIST our LORD of heaven and earth

Shake away the evil cash in on the rightous to see your own true worth

He waits for us to follow HIM away from this place

He will not leave us He is beyong time and space

His Adoptin Plan

Have you ever felt alone or cast out
Lingering over your feeling of anguish and doubt
No longer should you be left standing in the cold
There is ONE out there Who loves us all i am told
Do you feel this bitterness deep down to the bone
Or let others control you as you through life as a drone
You dont even have to stand in line to join HIS clan
For HE excepts us all with in HIS adoption plan
I reminded of a song that sings of a long black train
No more should you feel loneliness or pain
He is here waiting for us with open arms
No more man made security systems or silent alarms
He is our safety net our haven and our salvation
Just think of it as a peaceful and permanent vacation
We are still all HIS children which way we ran
We are forever HIS follow and walk with HIM for we are all apart of HIS
adoption plan

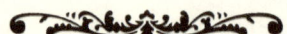

Let Him

you sit there alone pondering
in the darkness of your own thoughts
The words you seek are in the bible
HIS words will leave you full With no more wants
Bear the weight of your cross as you pass through this desert place
Ask for HIS guidance and forgiveness
for HE will wipe your slate clean leaving no trace
Bring glory to HIM
the maker of all you see
let HIM show you all HE has in store for you
as you bow down on bended knee
Let HIM open your eyes to the world around
as HE guides you along HIS path for you in life
He will never desert you or lead you astray
HE is there to lean on leaving behind all your worries and strife
He will bring you comfort
in your times of need letting you know he cares
Do not stress over all there is in this world let
HIM take over all your lifes affairs.

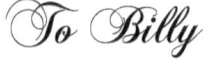

To Billy

Eyes of the Guardians

The softness of their voices comforts us
leaving a subtle feeling deep down inside
eyes that twinkle like evenings first star
smiles as bright as the trace of silvary moon
darkness disappears with them around
sent to us to guide us and keep us safe from harm
wings as white as a first days snow
the whisper of HIS truth and HIS bringers of peace
we sleep like children when they are near
giving us dreams so sweet taking away our fears
washing away all our worries and doubts
helping up to say the words we all know we must speak
always there to protect and guide us
still there when we cry and shout out for HIS help
they know that we are safe with GOD around
we believe in these heavenly angels
as they whisper to us from a distant echo
feeling our emotions and they know
all we in through guardians we shall call them
they are here for us in this life in all that we way do

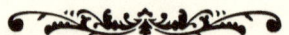

www.ingramcontent.com/pod-product-compliance
Lightning Source LLC
Chambersburg PA
CBHW022114170526
45157CB00004B/1638